Robbie the Raven
and Debbie the Dove

By: K.A. Mulenga

ROBBIE THE RAVEN AND DEBBIE THE DOVE

Published by Kalenga Augustine Mulenga

Johannesburg, South Africa

augustine@kamulenga.com

ISBN: 978-1-998954-50-6

eISBN: 978-1-998954-51-3

2 4 6 8 10 9 7 5 3 1

Illustration and layout by Boutique Books

Printed in South Africa by Bidvest Data

*I dedicate this book to my wife Sheba and my
kids, Grace, Malaika and Kalenga Jr.*

Thank you for believing in me!

*Thank you to Pamela Nomvete, whose generosity
has funded the publication of this book.*

Robbie the Raven and Debbie the Dove were best friends who loved to play together.

Every single day, they would fly high up into the sky and look down on all the people and the other animals of the world.

Debbie *loved* asking Robbie questions. **Every single day**, she would ask him things like:

"What are we doing today, Robbie?"

"Where are we going to fly today, Robbie?"

"What time are we going to eat today, Robbie?"

Robbie would answer all his best friend's questions. **Every single day**, he would answer her:

"We will go to the beach today, Debbie."

"We will fly over the forest today, Debbie."

"We will eat our worms at 12 o'clock, Debbie."

And that's why they were such good friends.

One day, Robbie and Debbie met up and, as usual, Debbie asked Robbie her questions:

"What are we doing today, Robbie?"

"Where are we going to fly today, Robbie?"

"What time are we going to eat today, Robbie?"

But, before Robbie could answer Debbie's questions, the two friends spotted four humans on the earth below them. The humans were walking along and carrying very heavy logs.

Robbie could tell that Debbie wanted to ask him what the humans were doing, because he knew that Debbie **loved** asking him questions.

But, before she could ask him anything, Robbie told her, *"That looks like Noah and his three sons. Noah is a good and faithful man and he loves God very much. Let's watch him and see what he is up to."*

Time went on, and Robbie and Debbie continued to watch Noah and his family from high up in the skies, **every single day**. They saw that the family were working very hard, **every single day**. They were building something together, something that got bigger and bigger and bigger, **every single day**.

Robbie told Debbie, *"I think God has told Noah to do something very important for Him."*

One day, Robbie and Debbie noticed that Noah and his family had finally stopped building. They were standing in front of an ark, which is an ***enormous*** type of boat. Noah and his family were telling all the animals to get into the ark that they had built, and the animals were all going inside, two by two.

Debbie was worried and now had a new question for Robbie.

"Look!" she cried. *"Don't you think we should get down there before we get left behind?"*

So, down they flew down to the ark, as quickly as they could. They made it into the ark just before Noah closed the doors!

Robbie and Debbie stayed on the boat with the rest of the animals.

They continued to play together, **every single day**, even though it was raining, **every single day**, and Debbie kept asking Robbie her questions, **every single day**.

But now, Debbie had a new set of questions for Robbie. She would ask him, **every single day**:

"How long are going to stay in this boat?"

"When are we going to be able to fly in the open air again?"

"Why is it raining so much?"

Robbie, always the patient one, explained to Debbie that God was not happy with the people on earth, because they were all doing very bad things. Noah was the only good man left on earth and that is why God had chosen him and his family to build the ark and rescue the animals.

Every single day, rain poured out of the skies and all the land was covered in water. But Robbie and Debbie and all the other animals were safe with Noah and his family in the ark. They waited and waited and waited in the ark for the rain to stop.

One day, after a very long time, the rain finally stopped. Noah opened a window and peered out. Then he called Robbie over to him and gave him a very important job to do. He asked him to fly over the earth until he could see that all the water on the land had dried up. Robbie flew back and forth, waiting to see when all the water on the land had dried up.

Then Noah gave Debbie a very important job to do too. He sent her out to see if she could find anywhere to rest her little feet. Debbie flew out to look, but she could not find any trees or any other place to rest her little feet and so she went back to Noah, who opened the window and let her back into the ark.

After seven days, Noah sent Debbie out again, to look for a place to rest her little feet. This time, Debbie found an olive tree which had new green leaves on its branches. She plucked a leaf from the tree and flew back to Noah, holding the leaf in her mouth all the way there. She gave Noah the leaf as proof that she had found a branch – a place where she could rest her little feet.

After another seven days, Noah sent Debbie out again. But this time, she didn't go back to Noah, because something wonderful happened.

When Debbie flew back to the olive tree, as she got closer to it, she saw someone who looked familiar.

It was her best friend, Robbie!

She started her questioning again.

"What time did you get here, Robbie?"

"What are we doing today, Robbie?"

"Where are we going to fly today, Robbie?"

"What time are we going to eat today, Robbie?"

Robbie smiled at Debbie and started answering all of her questions, just like he always did, **every single day**.

THE END

By K.A. Mulenga

Chuck the Cheetah

David, the great king

Donk and the Stubborn Donkeys

Elaine the Elephant

Four seasons in one day

Harry the Honest Horse

Imbwa, the Story Of the Dog and His Harsh Master

Joe Finds His Way Home

Max the Gorilla

Polly the Polecat

Robbie the Raven and Debbie the Dove

Spike and Spud , the Spaceboys

Susie Strickland, Sizzling Striker

The Leopard Licks Its Spots

The Lion and the Impala

The Weaver Birds

Will and His Best Friend Whale

Thank you for reading Robbie the Raven and Debbie the Dove.
I hope you enjoyed it! Please let K.A. Mulenga know about
what you thought about the book by leaving a short review on
Amazon, it will help other parents and children find the story.
(If you're under 13, ask a grown up to help you)

Top Tip: Be sure not to give away any of the story's secrets!

www.ingramcontent.com/pod-product-compliance
Lightning Source LLC
Chambersburg PA
CBHW042159030726
47599CB00004B/804